MONSTER GALAXY

MONSTER GALAXY

Cindy Veach

MoonPath Press

Copyright © 2025 Cindy Veach
All rights reserved.

No part of this publication may be reproduced, distributed,
or transmitted in any form or by any means whatsoever
without written permission from the publisher, except in
the case of brief excerpts for critical reviews and articles.
All inquiries should be addressed to MoonPath Press.

Poetry
ISBN 979-8-9899487-9-6

Cover Art: *Pallas Athene*, Gustav Klimt (1898)
oil on canvas, 75 × 75 cm
Vienna Museum, Austria
This work of art is in the public domain.

Author Photo: Rosanne Olson
www.rosanneolson.com

Book Design: Tonya Namura, using Malaga Narrow OTCE

MoonPath Press, an imprint of Concrete Wolf Poetry Series,
is dedicated to publishing the finest poets
living in the U.S. Pacific Northwest.

MoonPath Press
c/o Concrete Wolf

PO Box 2220
Newport, OR 97365-0163

MoonPathPress@gmail.com

http://MoonPathPress.com

for Carson and Ketner

A woman in the shape of a monster
a monster in the shape of a woman
the skies are full of them

—*Adrienne Rich*

Contents

A Partial Catalog of My Monsters	3

I

Girlhood	7
Even Now I'm Ashamed	8
Wanting	9
How I Negotiated My Childhood	11
Window	12
Because They Remind Me of My Mother's Dementia, I Throw Away the Pussy Willows	13
Self-Portrait as Daytime Television	14
Under My Bed	15
All Over Again	16
The Father's Daughter, Who Sprang from the Head of Zeus,	18
The Cardinal and His Song	19
The Ghost	21
Coming Out the Other Side of Winter	22

II

The Phantom Family	25
Challenger	26
I Think I Was a Good Daughter	28
Bulletproof	29
Lunar Tide	30
Ghost Letter	31
Some Things I Never Told Anyone	33
When They Said We Were Moving Again I Was Silent	36
Legacy	37

This Patch Where the Light Cannot Reach	38
Aglaecwif	40

III

Return to Earth	43
Mostly, I Thanked Him	44
The Age of Monsters	45
Seeing	46
While My High School Boyfriend Demonstrated How to Have Sex I Thought About Gravel Art	47
The Grand High Witch of All the World	48
All Birds Were Monsters Once	49
Being a Mother	50
Missing	51
Resolution	52
How to Recognize the Other Mother	54
The Gray	55
In Which I Submit to the Machine or Lies Told to the Good Girl	56
Alone in the High-Ceilinged Room	57
Letter to the Fog	58
Bumble	59
The Woman Who Swallowed a Python	60
Aubade	61

Notes	63
Acknowledgments	65
Gratitude	67
About the Author	69

MONSTER GALAXY

A Partial Catalog of My Monsters

One of my monsters is the flesh-eating Dimetrodon. One
is a giant chameleon with a twenty-foot tongue.

One takes the shape of a man with a dirk
in my girlhood bedroom. One is the Devil

Dementia who took his prehensile tentacle, pried
the latch and emptied my mother. One of my monsters

is The Good Girl. She's huge like a dirigible, huge
like the Jolly Green Giant. She can't pick up a pin,

can't make a move without wrecking her house.
One is The Other Mother. She slapped her child

for biting the baby she bled out to birth. Thus,
the monster called Shame. One is The Crone who begat

The Bone Vampire who feasts on spine, hip, femoral
neck. One is Forgetting, the other Remembering

she was a girl waving to her father leaving on a trip
his promise to bring her back little hotel soaps.

I

Girlhood

Penny Robinson was lost in space for three seasons.
I watched every single episode. I watched every single
Wednesday night on our RCA black-and-white TV
with tinfoil-wrapped rabbit ears. I watched Penny adopt
a Bloop and name it Debbie. I watched her accept shiny
crystals from Mr. Nobody. I watched a werewolf attack her.
I watched Sesmar put her feelings into his android
and Farnum, the evil zookeeper, add her to his human
collection. I watched the boy behind the mirror tell her
they could always have fun and stay children forever.
I watched her grow tall. I watched a girl with braids
and bangs become a beauty with breasts and a bob.
I watched and wanted to be her. I watched and stayed
short. I watched and stayed flat-chested. I watched
and stayed the good girl. I watched and was left behind.

Even Now I'm Ashamed

One slice of baloney between white bread
slicked with margarine, one navel orange.

I prayed for a trade-worthy brown-bag lunch.
I prayed for the miracle of a perfectly pressed

school uniform, knife pleats like the other girls.
Were my parents arguing over bills again?

Would Santa bring a navy blue, double-breasted
maxi coat like Laura's? Her grosgrain ribbons

and blonde pin curls. When I was a girl
alone in the dankness of our basement

I pushed a pussy willow catkin up my nose
to see if it would fit. No, I pushed myself

into the furred bud to see if I would fit.

Wanting

        Allen Ginsberg took a nap in my bedroom
before his reading at the college
where my father worked.
        Did he look in my closet,
desk drawers, read my diary—
      pages of secrets in Catholic girl cursive?
      When I babysat next door
I looked in the wife's closet, dozens of expensive
           dresses, tags still on.
    We were house poor. My clothes homemade.
      I wanted more.
I was infatuated with Twiggy, Cher, Veruschka,
   in love
      with Sidney Poitier—
  sang "To Sir, with Love" into my hairbrush.
I thought I had a voice.
     I believed
I'd be discovered.
       Instead, Ginsberg
in my girlhood bedroom
maybe getting high, meditating, chanting.
    What is proximity worth by itself?
    I recall his unkempt beard,
where he sat at our dinner table
        but not a word he said.

What happened to that crosshair of time?
    The next year brought
        the Summer of Love, riots, assassinations,
    my menarche, menarche, menarche—
         vermilion stains
on snow-white sheets.
    When does a childhood end?
        After two hundred clover chains, fifty
root beer floats? I find our old house on Zillow,
close my eyes, picture my room—
    ivory walls, second-hand furniture, floral spread.

How I Negotiated My Childhood

I pretend to nap at my birthday party. Hide under a blanket
        spread on patchy grass, wrap it over my skin
and green blades. I want to disappear

                and be the center of attention.

        I peek out. See the girls invited from school
running, playing tag, pumping their legs on swings
        all curls and crinoline.

           I'm not like them

my home-made pedal pushers
        our overgrown yard: weeds and weeds
around the rental house.

           I hide my head.

        Dad's studying for his BA, works night shift
at the Union Leader. Mom picks the meat
        off chicken necks for supper.

           I keep still.

The ground so damp
        mosquitoes enter my room at night
tears in the window screens.

           I hide my head.

        Everyone plays around me.
I'm five and forty and sixty-eight.
        I'm not like other girls.

           I watch them eating cake.

Window

The furnace works overtime
          while sunlight paints

                    bright bars
on polished hardwood.

This whole country gripped
          by bitter cold

                    even the South
where I'm a visitor.

In the first house I remember
          one window held

                    a lintel transom
of leaded glass.

Prisms flew around that room—
          violet, indigo, blue, green, yellow, orange, red—

                    gracing every member of my family
reaching the darkest corners,

even dust motes
          sparkled like something precious.

                    This held no meaning for me.
I was not familiar

          with the way things will end.

Because They Remind Me of My Mother's Dementia, I Throw Away the Pussy Willows

For two years they sat with me at the Formica table,
ate with me, read with me, wrote with me. But today,
when I look at them, I see cobwebs connecting
one catkin to the next and then they turn into furry
Cossack hats and the photo of my mother wearing one
when they were the rage in the sixties. She can't remember
where she was, which two children were at her side.
I fear this. I touch one of the catkins and it falls off.
I touch another and it falls off. These stems denied water,
not allowed to bloom, have lived in a time warp,
a perpetual spring—a trove of vintage hats, an eternally
budding army standing at attention—my lost mother,
forever stylish and beautiful in her beloved Cossack cap.

Self-Portrait as Daytime Television

It's like the days sped away and now here I am
left with the memory of Morticia Addams twirling
her long black tresses. It's as if I lost my baby brother
the day he toddled into the bee's nest and not years later
after a hundred benders ruined his heart. It's as if
the hours sped away and here I am left with the memory
of JFK—and me, weeping over pictures of Jackie in *Look*,
asking how she could marry Ari Onassis. It's as if my
half-century of raising kids turned into one day and now
I'm left with the memory of the spearmint my mother
planted behind our house. It's like some days got stuck—
here I am again, in the TV room, *Dark Shadows*
and the red wall-to-wall shag—while others snuck away.
It's as if I lost the diary with the blue cover, the lock,
the key and now I'm left with the memory of my father
forever holding my brother, running across the lawn
shouting, "Start the car," and the stupid way
the Three Stooges slapped each other silly Saturday
mornings in black-and-white.

Under My Bed

I put a photo of my brother on the night-
stand, but I found it hard to look at him.
It's the last photo. His hair short, tight
curls buzzed off—not how I remember him.

There's a yellow dog in this photo. Not his.
Whose dog? How can I not know my brother?
What happened after he left home? His
right hand on the dog's broad head. The other

outside the frame. Haven't we all lost
brothers one way or another? I know
where this is headed, the hidden cost,
generational, impossible to stop. I know.

He was sober for months his sponsor said.
I put the photo back in the box under my bed.

All Over Again

I remember and tell it
    to downed leaves rattling

across the patio, scraping
    together in the trees

then look away
    toward the pond—its calm denial—

its promise of bass,
    a small boat, oars.

These days I measure time
    by what is gone—

a year ago this, a year ago that.
    It's the brittle season.

Each gust wills more leaves down,
    shivers the pond's surface—

while underneath painted turtles, bullfrogs, mayflies
    dig themselves into muck.

It's warm. It's cold,
    I find the one beam

of sunlight,
    shadows across the page.

Out of nowhere
    a burying beetle

lands on its back, buzzes—
    I've lost my one father—

how dare you carry on
    as if nothing has happened.

The Father's Daughter, Who Sprang from the Head of Zeus,

shall respect her father's jewelry phobia and wait until
she's eighteen to pierce her ears, shall respect her father's
phobia of touching the soles of shoes for where have they
been? (on sidewalks where people have __, in restrooms
where people have __), shall jump up from the table, clear
the dishes, wash the dishes, shall be his prep cook, his sous-
chef, mincing garlic, chopping onions, scrubbing clams,
cleaning squid (removing the cartilage, beak, ink sac—
blue-black seeping into her cuticles), shall get good grades
(but not be as smart as her older brother, the firstborn),
shall not speak up at the dinner table, shall let her father
and brother discuss Nixon, the draft, the body count, shall
pretend (while at a beach where women in string bikinis are
sunbathing) that she doesn't hear her father say to her
brother (the firstborn) *let's go check out the merchandise,*
shall be plain (while her sister shall be a beauty and break
all the makeup, jewelry, dating rules), shall not be jealous,
shall not complain, shall not disappoint, shall take
the blame, shall bite her tongue, shall swallow the blood.

The Cardinal and His Song

The cardinal sang out when I fumbled for my phone
     and for the first time I connected this bird

with that song. It was like I learned a new word, like a light—

     I didn't get a picture of the cardinal.
He crossed the street for another tree. Wait,

there's something missing in this story.
                           Let me go back and start over.

My father never told me he loved me. He could not speak
     those words.

Now, I'll know the cardinal by his song. Okay,

this is just one part of the story that was missing:
              until you know something you have no idea—

If I said *I love you,* my father would say, *Right back at you.*
Until the day he died I hoped he'd say—I'm sorry

     but part of this story is still missing. For a moment
on the sidewalk when I connected

                   the cardinal with his song I wondered,

is this what could have been? This felt like
walking on the edge of an envelope so I'm afraid

I just added a little blood to this story.
    Make no mistake. From here on out I will know him

                                by that song.

    What else have I missed?
Hold on. Let me go back. I think I need to start over.

The Ghost

I ran into my father's ghost at the supermarket fish
display. Squid + colossal shrimp + cherrystones = his
famous paella. I try not to shop with him in my head.
Everyday we have these little battles going on inside us. Soak
clams in cornmeal water. Remove squid beak. Generous pinch
of saffron. Jasmine rice. *What we want to do, and what
we need to do, sometimes they can be very different things.*
You must scorch the planet in a cast-iron skillet and eat
the burnt underside like a communal offering. *I will hate
you for not loving me enough to stay.* Even the clams
I bought are still breathing. They spit stars in my face
when I open their shells.

Coming Out the Other Side of Winter

Grief repeats itself a thousand different ways.
Water runs, glistens down the rock face.
Jonquils, crocus, hyacinth, poke their faithful heads
up from the dirt. Once I believed
but monsters took root in me.
Now my pockets fill with empty. Now sadness wraps
my neck, hangs off my shoulders—a heavy old sweater,
woolen, hand-wash only. So many tender petals unfurling.
And those earnest blossoms of trees—
the magnolia, cherry, dogwood.
Here too, in the mown field, its stacked bales.
In the nest of mud and straw, three blue eggs.
In a cloud's chrysalis of familiar faces.
In my eyes, throat, all down my crumbling spine—
vertebrae, vertebrae, vertebrae.

II

II

The Phantom Family

Never love anything, kiddo, you will just end up losing it.
                                            —*Penny Robinson*

Alien fog blinded us when solar winds gusted when the compass needle shivered *Warning! Warning!* when charged particles battered our nuclear ship when dad was at the wheel when mom was confirming coordinates—*We're lost, aren't we?* when I leaned on my sister who leaned on our brother *Don't leave me alone* when the hum of the car when their muffled voices when we fell asleep when we felt safe when we had parents when we fell asleep when we felt safe when we had parents when the hum of the car when their muffled voices *Don't leave me alone* when I leaned on my sister who leaned on our brother *We're lost aren't we?* when mom was confirming coordinates when charged particles battered our nuclear ship when dad was at the wheel *Warning! Warning!* when the compass needle shivered when alien fog blinded us when solar winds gusted.

Challenger

Three decades later I return
to where I once lived

and drive the twenty miles,
Port Ludlow to Port Townsend,

past the spot I was passing—
driving our old gray bug

eight months pregnant with my first—
when the news came over the radio.

News I strained to hear, twisting the dial,
thinking first of the teacher astronaut, a young

mother of two. And then, of my unborn child,
safe, contained. In fact, he was kicking me,

seat belt pressing into us. And then,
I kept driving toward my appointment,

toward my own motherhood. I kept on driving
as the capsule was falling, as the teacher's

children, husband, parents stood in the stands
watching. It turns out the crew was alive

the whole time the vessel was descending,
hurtling toward home, toward the waiting water.

Would knowing this have changed anything?
All these years, I've been guilty

of nothing but happiness.
Conifer clouds, sneak peeks of sky.

I Think I Was a Good Daughter

A man so allergic to what he caught—
              I had to bait his hooks, unhook his catch.

I touched the worms. I pierced their bodies.
    I touched the fish

    flapping and fighting the barb
and every time he asked, I cleaned his fish, slit

    each one with a steak knife, lifted
the tiny heart and liver and entrails

            up with the tip of the blade.

A man who loved the ocean,
    the idea of fishing, surf casting,

            whose tackle box was a disaster
of tangled line, rusted reels.

I don't know how it happens that a big man,
    a man so present,
             lies down and lies down—

    anymore than a sky can shed
        itself of sky—

After I touched his face for the last time
    after I touched down in Boston
              after I made it home

    I was as alone as a cornered spider.

Why am I telling you this?

Bulletproof

    Before my belly was a kiln. Before episiotomy.
Before hemorrhage. Years before my brother started spiking
his thermos with Absolut. Before my mother forgot. Before
my father died, Al Hirschfeld hid his daughter's name

    in drawings of Marilyn, Elvis, Ella, Ringo Starr.
NINAs concealed in gams and jowls. *Harmless insanity* he
called it. Long before I left the church. Before my children
left home. And yes, it's true that the army used Al's NINAs

    to train bomber pilots to spot their targets. And yes,
I've now lived long enough to know what I did not know
then—that he objected to his art being used to kill people,
drew his daughter with no NINAs and named it

    Nina's Revenge; that some nights my father
took off to wander Times Square, eat at an Automat—
or so he said. And yes, maybe my brother was right
that he wasn't always true—but some memories

    are bulletproof. I look back and long for the Sundays
my father came home with bagels and the *The New York Times*
and we'd spend all morning searching for the NINAs
in that week's Hirschfeld drawing.

Lunar Tide

When the rising tide catches me, I pause and watch the crest
and crash. One minute it pushes me against the rocks,
makes me walk in soft sand, gravity pulling my shoes deep
down, crushing my shoreline and the next minute, it pulls
back, releases me, lets me walk the hard sand, walk
weightless to the far end of the beach—pink kelp, startled
crabs, shell glitter. I want to blame the moon, but there is
no tide table for this. Home, at the end of my evening walk

I salt boiling broth
watch the gas burner flicker
my breath turns to steam.

Ghost Letter

I didn't think of you today
    or maybe I did once

on the car ride back
    from hiking Oxbow Loop

where I learned that water,
    separated from its source,

silts up, evaporates.
    This place is moss-hung, hemmed

with old growth.
    The only birds I saw were corvids

and whenever I stopped
    mosquitoes found me.

Near the halfway point
    I took a spur trail to the river

where the dog waded out
    across slick boulders.

I swear
    I can't even remember

what thought it was
    I had of you

but what I do remember
    is choosing not to speak it.

The world you built for me
    is evaporating. Today,

I saw the way the river
    kept pushing past this oxbow,

choosing the forward path,
    loving each stone, spilling

over them with what I can only
    call delight. Don't be surprised,

you knew it would come to this, you
    who always leaned toward darkness,

evenings, silent in your easy chair,
    sipping cabernet, listening to opera.

Some Things I Never Told Anyone

    When I begged my parents
to let me go on the Mousetrap ride
    I didn't know
that at each and every hairpin turn
    half my car would hang
for what seemed minutes in midair
    before jerking right or left
then back
    to a too-short straightaway
before the next turn
    and the next
why did I tell them I loved it

    On that holiday when my father
forgot the Nikon
    its rolls and rolls of 35mm film
all our vacation photos
    on the hook of a stall door
in a London men's room
    remembered
when we were in the Tube
    hurtling toward Heathrow
he lost his temper yelled at us
    why did I think it was my fault

I picked that coaster ride
    to show my parents
that their preteen daughter
    could go it alone
dizzy with shame
    white-knuckled
I spotted them
    far below on trusted ground
clung to their faces

    Why did I keep it to myself
when we stayed that night
    at the highway motel
room doors open to the outdoors
    and I was helping
carry our stuff board games piled
    to my chin
and lost my way
    picked the wrong door
pushed with my foot
    and walked in
on a naked couple limbs entwined
    the woman looked right at me
all those game boxes
    Chutes and Ladders Candy Land Life
each sharp edge marking
    the tender insides of my forearms

My father left us standing there in the London Tube
    six kids my mother her massive canvas bag
of passports snacks tickets
    the woman looked right at me
pulled the white sheet over their tangled legs
    I could not turn away
I'd never seen my parents touch
    I gripped that Mousetrap's safety bar
he caught the next train back
    to that stop that men's room
the camera gone
    I saw I saw I saw
they were grown-ups
    as beautiful as statues in museums
and I still blame myself

When They Said We Were Moving Again I Was Silent

And I'm silent when asked where I'm from, where I grew up.
I think of the forest behind the rented house where
I played bandits with my brother and we dragged rickety
wooden sleds in winter. I think of that one year
in Watertown, walking to kindergarten in the rain, yellow
slickers, holding my brother's hand. I think of IU's married
student housing, its collage of kids, blocks of concrete
sidewalks, how there was a roller-skating gang, and I wore
a key around my neck. I think of how my parents sat us
down to announce each move: Indiana to New York. And
the row of arborvitaes my father planted, root balls
wrapped in burlap, watered each night until the next move:
New York to Iowa. Same old caravan: two used cars, over
packed, riding low, one U-Haul trailer with jury-rigged
brake lights. Furthest west I'd ever been. Another chance
to reinvent myself? Tell me, what is it to be grounded,
to be from a place?

In Iowa fields
of corn and soybean stubble
hidden trilobites.

Legacy

I don't know what happened
        to the cast-iron skillets my father collected

              from thrift shops around Chicago—
rusted, in need of steel wool, olive oil, heat.

When I come across cast-iron sets
        in the Vermont Country Store catalog

              I turn the page. It's raining, gloomy
but there's a Snow Moon coming—

a welcome respite from the darkness.
        My father was overprotective, paranoid—

              dead bolt, door chain, secret knock—
no place was safe. I was afraid to go anywhere alone,

afraid of my shadow. He left me
        before the discovery of a rare monster galaxy—

              a massive blaze of suns that spawned
in the early universe then died. Even now, its dark matter

looms in the cosmos, isolated,
        no longer birthing stars. If there is life after death

              what is this galaxy's fate?
I followed his instructions to a T—

and yet, his carbon, his dust. Will I ever know
        what happened to those skillets?

              Their constellation of crumbs,
congealed grease, droplets of condensation quivering.

This Patch Where the Light Cannot Reach

I see a candelabra of branches
or birds

crossing landscapes
flickering above fences

laying rails down
on so-white snow

on cold so cold.
That tatted freight train

flashing past, shadowboxing
tunnel, trestle

approaching Minneapolis,
or any city's welcome mat

of skyscraper penumbras.
I see if I sit on a park bench

in memory of,
a late afternoon in winter

black stripes like a zebra
on the loose.

And a can of pop someone left—
its dark ellipse. Its crush.

I see ducks casting
over the iced millpond

below the Malt-O-Meal plant.
Low banks of stubble and freeze.

Shadow's shadow
of daddy longlegs. Oh

to be a thing that doesn't subscribe
to age

or gender.
I tissue its delicate legs.

I crush. There was supposed to be
a father in this poem.

Aglaecwif

Outside my window men are repainting the crosswalk
putting new lines over old lines.

I learned a new word today, an Old English word—
aglaecwif—a monster-woman, troll-lady, wretch, hag.

Think, The Grand High Witch of All the World.
Think, Grendel's no-name mother.

And then I learned that this word aglaecwif
is the feminine form of aglaeca: a hero,

a valiant warrior. Why am I not surprised? I know
these tropes: the monster mother, the sexless crone—

toothy, bald, clawed, toeless child-hater, child-eater.
If all witches are women as Roald Dahl wrote

then I claim that pedigree but explain why gender
makes me witch not warrior, hag not hero. What

patriarchal alchemy creates monsters out of what
I'm supposed to be versus what I am?

I have tried to be good, to exist between the lines
yet look at me, my galaxy of monsters.

III

Return to Earth

It doesn't mean you can't try to understand about fathers.
—Penny Robinson

Stars on earth are famous humans, starfish, star fruit, good
girl gold stars and the stars I learned to draw without lifting
pen from paper—one continuous line—the way my father
taught me. How I still draw them. He taught me one joke:
What's black and white and red (read) all over? He taught
me falling stars aren't stars but tiny cosmic rocks burning
up as they hit our atmosphere. Stick figures. Lollipop trees.
Lopsided stars. This isn't a fraction of who he was on earth.
I'm not letting go of satellite memories: his deathbed's
reflection in the spaceship's titanium steel, my last attempts
to feed his ego—*this, leader of my planet*—scrambled eggs,
a side of gratitude, two bites before the plate went cold
on the nightstand beside his morphine, his oxygen.

Mostly, I Thanked Him

Tonight, I misread dish towel as death towel—
white with stitched skull and crossbones,

adorned with nightshade, hemlock embroidered
in purple thread, silk. There's a terrible wind

stealing the neighborhood's recycling, dragging it
down sidewalks. Birds shelter in place

all but invisible as I sit here staring at a bouquet
of pussy willows, thinking about Keats—

his lock of hair in a crooked cabinet, the plaster death
mask, how they burned everything but that ceiling—

sky blue, white medallions. I say funicular out loud—
like funnel, like ocular, like familiar, like fun.

What I remember is never what others remember.
I rode the Duquesne Incline up the mountainside

with my father. We went up, we went down—it was slow,
I was impatient; it was long before I misread death towel.

Up, down, up, down without questioning the mechanics:
ropes, counterbalance. The day my father died

I told him everything I wanted to tell him.

The Age of Monsters

There's one bird
that every evening
calls and calls
that I can't seem
to locate

but I've grown used
to lying here listening
trying to imagine
her level of lust
at dusk.

Truth might be the night
coming on to me
putting the body to bed
by itself.

I lift up my nightgown
this body
untouched
for years
slips from it.

Pound for pound
I am more crone
less girl.

I look down at myself
my unsung flesh
I'll never be that shameless bird.

Seeing

Across the street   the trunk   of a small tree

        has a long opening   where the bark curls

back exposing

        labia vagina vulva.

Rain   for two days   soft as a veil

        her opening

        a patina of verdigris green

curves away

        then reunites at the seams

        the lower seam leads   to the earth

and the upper

        to a constellation of branches

their tongue-shaped leaves   turning now

        into tiny flames on stems.

Does anyone else see me?

While My High School Boyfriend Demonstrated How to Have Sex I Thought About Gravel Art

He took me to his bedroom, lay down
on me, gently, both of us fully clothed.

While he moved and moaned, I eyed the window,
ceiling, daydreamed. Iowa winters were barren,

roads frozen into their gravel. Most days
I stayed inside turning colored grit and glue

into warmer scenes: palms, sparkly atolls,
leggy shrimp, clown fish. He was heavier

than he looked, held his breath tight.
Six months going steady. All my girlfriends

having sex. I couldn't care less,
felt nothing, felt numb.

The Grand High Witch of All the World

She is the woman in the mirror
      inspecting a bruise.
She is the bruise on a fallen
      apple and its shame.
She is ashamed of her body
      flaws and crocodile skin.
She is covering up her skin,
      secrets as numerous as starlings.

She is a kettle of secrets
      and ancient sins and yes
She is ancient
      a coven of too-muchness and yes
She is called hag for being herself
      bald with blue spittle and a pointy, black hat.
She is a hat trick of monsters
      scanty eyebrows, neck folds, bone tears.

She is the child who failed at math, tears
      at the blackboard in front of the class.
She is the girl from a lower class
      who still remembers her one new dress.
She is the one who would not raise her dress
      for him or him and was called prude.
Prude, because she did not feel desire
      because she would never be enough.

All Birds Were Monsters Once

When I hate this body
I remind myself
of the abandoned nest
of mud and straw
way up in the lilac bush
of every bird
all throat and call
refusing to be silenced
and what was never
mine to keep.

Being a Mother

When I first put her on
she fit me to a T.
And looking back
I can see her
reflection in the full-length
pushing you in an umbrella stroller
as you cuddled
your Gund bunny.
The minute you were grown
she shed me
the way a snake
sloughs skin.
What kind of mother
trick is that?
Deep down
in my gut of guts
I want you
to know me
as I am
and be okay—
meanwhile
I walk behind you
on a path
through your new neighborhood
stopping to wonder
at some flowers
I can't name
because I'll never be
that person again—
something tall
with purple bulbs, thistlelike
studded with dormant bees.

Missing

    When my body no longer contained his
I made a point of taking him out to the sandy spit
where I walked days he was becoming somebody.
I won't say when god was making him—mouth,
eyes, limbs, heart—because I can now admit
I don't believe, the way I can now admit this:
I didn't recognize myself after his body left my body.
    At the spot where the Sound wraps around
the point—where loose logs, deadheads, culls
once washed up from the old Pope & Russell
sawmill—there's now a fancy inn, condos. I missed
the flutter, even his sharp ankles, or was it a fist,
between my ribs. A thousand iridescent mussel
shells, split open, soft bodies pilfered by gulls.

Resolution

        Rain-slick morning,
yellow light of a road crew truck
here to fill winter potholes
strobing through the gray.
Migraine monster—I know my triggers.

        Know to look away from this light
and the sadness of the chained
farm stand entrance—memories of ripe peaches,
Gravensteins, noble firs, kissing balls—
and focus on negotiating the gym parking lot
packed with New Year's resolution makers.

        Know to find joy in photos of winter
jasmine and the hot new lover my friend in the South
posts this frigid January. Take pride in the soup
I made last night. Spicy and flush with shrimp—
my guests smacked their lips and asked for more.
Still, even all these years after menopause,
there are nights I do not sleep.

        My body's gone soft. Limbs ache
but I keep this to myself. I miss my kids. Yet,
a stiff wind rushing down the street
giving the trees no choice but to move
brings a nod when it blows down

a neighbor's privacy fence
revealing sculptures
of naked couples.

        My hand-me-down orchid
has two buds, two nipples about to unfold.
I am still blooming—

How to Recognize the Other Mother

She's a smidge too long in the tooth.
Her gray hair snakes around her head.
Her eyes are brown and flat as buttons.

She will say *why don't you sit down.*
You will say *I didn't know I had another mother.*
She will say *everyone does.*

She will tell you that for years she was cloaked
in the invisibility of maternal love,
that for years there was nothing

but you, only you, and she was all in.
She will say she loves you and wants you
to know her but will offer no instructions.

And you will sit there. And you will notice
she is shorter than she was. Her skin lined,
papery. Her fingernails yellow, brittle.

And, for the first time, you will see her
like dust motes in a beam of light.

The Gray

You make me think of pewter, sticky on the inside
thrift shop pitchers—all those years of accumulated

gunk that no sponge or bottle brush can reach.
You make me think of heavy sowbelly skies,

100% humidity—the weighty weight of it all.
Gray, you are the antithesis of bougainvillea,

cheery saccharine packets, gyrating disco
balls. You are a stinking hot breeze

rifling the old neighborhood. You are wilting
breasts, senile angiomas, vaginitis, osteoporosis.

Oh, little bitty gray moth plastered to the gray doorframe
who thought yourself invisible—I see you

and raise you three parts 506 to one part 505
to equal parts peroxide.

In Which I Submit to the Machine or Lies Told to the Good Girl

The scan—in which they check
the amount of mineral density
in the lumbar spine, left hip, right hip
as if I'm some kind of deeply dug,
excavated, exhausted, robbed-
of-riches mine about to calve its scaffolding—
is painless. Like me, the machine is silent
and white. It glides over my body
without touching my body—a benevolent
hand assessing my aging ramparts.
I do my part. Lie exactly as instructed.
Lie hands at my sides. Lie
like the good girl I am—knees up
on the Plexiglas block, ankles turned
out, tied in place, tight, but not too tight.

Alone in the High-Ceilinged Room

My fan clicks each time it completes
an orbit. I've opened all the windows

so the mid-August heat can sit with me.
There's just enough breeze for pines

on the boulevard to talk among themselves.
Two teen boys, shouldering overstuffed

backpacks, speed by in loud conversation,
peddling standing up. My kids are three thousand

miles away, three hours behind me. Right now,
he's getting behind the wheel; she's catching a ferry,

both headed into their workday. Once, being alone
for an afternoon was as elusive as the quetzal bird.

What naps? He was colicky. Then, she came along
and needed my breast. And when she needed my breast

he needed my lap. Unseen starlings chitter away.
Whatever they're saying is not meant for me.

Nor is the joy of those boys my joy. By now,
they've thrown their bikes and backpacks down,

stripped off their t-shirts, jumped into a friend's pool.
I'm on a different planet, orbiting a new sun

and there's the slightest breeze whispering—
what's next what's next what's next.

Letter to the Fog

The air is thick with you.
Trees drip, drip, drip with you.

I'm wearing what I slept in.
The book on my lap gone limp

with you. A lady cardinal
lands on the oilcloth

where last night, under a strawberry
moon and Venus, I shelled a lobster

I let the supermarket kill.
Sweet meat, ruby roe.

A ferry blows one long low note—
you, you, you—

I love an anchor,
but I will not partner again.

I'm happy here alone
swathed in your all-night dress.

Bumble

I don't send signals that I want. I'm not
that bird with the bright feathers or elegant neck
getting all the attention at the feeder. I'm not
that flirty hummingbird sipping a sweet
red cocktail. I look away from the mirror.
Choose not to vie for cracked seeds, sugar water.
All those mean bees lying in wait
with their yellow jackets, their buzz.
Sure, I've heard there are benevolent ones
drones who mate and do not sting. Convince me.
I'm a poor apiarist, Queen of Mistakes—
errant toxin under the skin, the hunt
for the elusive stinger. If one comes at me
I will swarm. I will swat. I will squash.
I'm becoming what no man or woman wants,
a hive of my own making.

The Woman Who Swallowed a Python

A woman went into her cornfield and swallowed a python.
The cobs were frightened. Even wild boars ran away.
Inside every woman there are monsters. A woman can
swallow and swallow. She can choke down her truth
for a hundred reasons. Unzip her and meet the beasts.
Follow my footsteps. Here are the things you will need:
flashlight, slippers, machete. Come alone. If you're lucky
you will find her. There will be questions. Can a woman
choke down shame? Can a woman choke down her bones,
her mind? There will be speculation. Who swallowed
whom? Is there a woman inside every monster or monsters
inside every woman? What if both things can be true.
A reticulation of wrinkles and collagen, wisdom
and faux pas, fear and ferocity.

Aubade

Spring frost on the windshield, fingerprint whorls, lace—
        I scrape and scrape.

A block away, bells start up at the Baptist church
        with the white picket fence.

It's too cold for April, blinding sun
        glances off the glass

and I am done—
        will squint through what remains

as I drive north and east, Gloucester, Rockport.
        In Catholic school I learned

that the soul was a sphere, milky
        like a full moon, and every sin

a black speck—kettle of invasive starlings.
        The habited sisters made us count and catalog

every wrong
        only god could absolve.

Sunday mornings I go to the sea—
        I have done the best I can.

Notes

The epigraph for "Monster Galaxy" is reprinted by permission of W. W. Norton & Company, Inc. Copyright Credit: Adrienne Rich, "Planetarium" from *Collected Poems: 1950–2012*. Copyright © 2016 by The Adrienne Rich Literary Trust. Copyright © 1971 W. W. Norton & Company, Inc.

"A Partial Catalog of My Monsters" borrows from and was inspired by the poem "Genealogy" by Betsy Sholl.

The line "When does a childhood end?" in the poem "Wanting" is from "Kyrie" by Ellen Bryant Voigt.

"Ghost Letter" was inspired by the poem "Letter" by Bob Bradshaw.

"This Patch Where the Light Cannot Reach" takes its title from: *http://kinooze.com/what-is-a-shadow/*

The poem "Aglaecwif" borrows from and was inspired by Susan Rich's poem "Boketto" and this quote from *Women and Other Monsters* by Jess Zimmerman: "Monsters are created in the difference between what we are supposed to be and what we are."

The lines "I am more crone / less girl" in the poem "The Age of Monsters" was inspired by the line "...(less girl than gnome)" in the poem "Dear Mother," from the book *Yours, Creature* by Jessica Cuello.

The poem "The Grand High Witch of All the World" borrows from and was inspired by the poem "Portrait with Closed Eyes" by Jeanne Marie Beaumont and the novel *The Witches* by Roald Dahl.

The poem "How to Recognize the Other Mother" takes its inspiration from the novel *Coraline* by Neil Gaiman.

"The Woman Who Swallowed a Python" was inspired by a Yahoo! News story, "Woman Swallowed by Python as She Checked on Her Cornfield," The Editors, April 25, 2021, https://www.yahoo.com/lifestyle/woman-swallowed-python-she-checked-100000564.html.

The poems "The Ghost," "The Phantom Family," and "Return to Earth" incorporate dialog (in italics) from the television series *Lost in Space*.

Acknowledgments

Grateful acknowledgment is made to the following journals in which these poems, or versions of these poems, first appeared.

Anti-Heroin Chic: "Under My Bed"

Atticus Review: "Challenger"

Connecticut River Review: "Legacy"

Gold Man Review: "Aglaecwif"

The Indianapolis Review: "Alone in the High-Ceilinged Room"

Lily Poetry Review: "A Partial Catalog of My Monsters"

Nixes Mate Review: "Because They Remind Me of My Mother's Dementia, I Throw Away the Pussy Willows"

The Ocean State Review: "All Over Again"

On the Seawall: "The Cardinal and His Song"

ONE ART: a journal of poetry: "Bulletproof"

Presence: A Journal of Catholic Poetry: "Coming Out the Other Side of Winter"

Quartet Journal: "Missing"

Rattle: "Some Things I Never Told Anyone"

Rogue Agent: "In Which I Submit to the Machine or Lies Told to the Good Girl," "The Woman Who Swallowed a Python"

Salt Hill Journal: "This Patch Where the Light Cannot Reach" (2019 Philip Booth Poetry Prize selected by Mary Ruefle)

Spillway: "Mostly, I Thanked Him" (reprinted in *Incessant Pipe*)

The Stirring: "All Birds Were Monsters Once" (reprinted in *Poems to Go*)

Stone Canoe: "Aubade"

SWWIM: "The Gray"

UCity Review: "The Ghost"
The Worcester Review: "Window"
Yellow Chair Review: "Being a Mother"

Gratitude

Thank you to MoonPath Press and Lana Hechtman Ayers for bringing *Monster Galaxy* into the world with kindness and care.

So much love to my East Coast poetry family: Kathi Aguero, Kevin Carey, M.P. Carver, Richard Hoffman, Elisabeth Weiss Horowitz, Jennifer Jean, Danielle Jones, K.T. Landon, Kali Lightfoot, Jennifer Martelli, Colleen Michaels, Rebecca Hart Olander, January Gill O'Neil, Carla Panciera, Dawn Paul, J.D. Scrimgeour and to my West Coast poetry family: Kelli Russell Agodon, Subhaga Crystal Bacon, Christine Balk, Michele Bombardier, Suzanne Edison, Katy Ellis, John Harn, Susan Landgraf, Susan Rich and Heidi Seaborn. Your friendship and community are everything.

Very special thanks to Susan Rich for her astute editorial help with *Monster Galaxy* and to the Good Harbor poets (K. T. Kali, Jenn, Carla, Becky) for their suggestions and especially to Jenn Martelli for her ordering witchcraft.

I am forever grateful to dear, lifelong friends: Carol, Cynthia, Jane and Susan B.

To my brother, Carson, and sister, Cathy, together we are stronger.

In memory of my parents whom I miss beyond words.

And to my children, Carson and Ketner, my greatest loves, always and forever.

About the Author

Cindy Veach is the author of three full-length poetry collections: *Monster Galaxy* (MoonPath Press), a finalist for the Sally Albiso Award; *Her Kind* (CavanKerry Press), an Eric Hoffer Montaigne Medal finalist; and *Gloved Against Blood* (CavanKerry Press), a finalist for the Paterson Poetry Prize and a Massachusetts Center for the Book "Must Read." She is also the author of the chapbook *Innocents* (Nixes Mate Press) and co-author, with J. D. Scrimgeour, of the script *Imprisoned! 1692* produced by the Essex National Heritage Commission. Her poems have appeared in the Academy of American Poets Poem-a-Day series, *AGNI, Michigan Quarterly Review, North American Review, Poet Lore, Salamander, Verse Daily*, and elsewhere. A recipient of the Philip Booth Poetry Prize (selected by Mary Ruefle) and the Samuel Allen Washington Prize (selected by Marilyn Nelson), she is poetry co-editor of *MER*.

Cindy received an MFA from the University of Oregon where she was a graduate teaching fellow and an assistant poetry editor for *Northwest Review*. She has been a workshop instructor, a panelist at poetry festivals, and served as a reader and judge for poetry contests.

After living on Boston's North Shore (Cape Ann) for thirty years, Cindy now resides in the Seattle area.

www.ingramcontent.com/pod-product-compliance
Lightning Source LLC
LaVergne TN
LVHW041629070526
838199LV00052B/3292